15 Offline 1
Strategies

by Alex Genadinik

ISBN:151936976X
ISBN-13: 978-1519369765

DEDICATION

Dedicated to my mother and grandmother who are the biggest entrepreneurs I know.

CONTENTS

13. Direct snail mail advertising
14. Setting up a storefront
15. Fairs and flea markets

Further resources and free gifts to help you

1. 3 Free gifts for you
2. Additional resources that will help you with your events and overall business

FORWARD

The advice in this book is based on my own experience and success promoting my business with the following offline marketing strategies. In sharing them, my hope is that you too will find success, and be able to grow your business using these techniques. I wish you the best of luck in your business and hope that the ideas in this book can contribute to your success. Enjoy the book.

Before we start

A VERY WARM WELCOME TO YOU

Hello, I am excited that you got this book, and I want to extend a very warm welcome to you. In writing this book I did my best to cover every element that I think will help you get the most out of your offline marketing efforts.

I hope you enjoy the book, and I hope to hear from you when you finish it. Whether you like the book or not, I'd love to hear your thoughts on how the book currently is, and how you think it can be improved. My email address is alex.genadinik@gmail.com and I look forward to hearing from you after you complete the book.

Why the book is so short: this is a relatively short book, but it is VERY to the point. My aim was to keep it short and sweet so that you can quickly get through it, not get bogged down reading things you don't need, and be able to quickly start implementing the strategies in the book.

GIFTS FOR YOU

As I mentioned, I am excited that you got the book and I want to make sure that you really get a lot of value from this book.

At the end of the book there are 3 additional resources that I made free for you for free. There are also a number of very discounted resources listed there that might help you. The reason they are discounted and not free is that it just isn't possible for me to give everything away for free. But I did provide very big discounts to make it almost free. Browse all the resources there, and definitely take advantage of the free gifts from me.

While writing this book I debated whether to add the paid/discounted products. I realize that it might be off putting for you to be sold additional products. What I decided in the end is to only add paid products if they are REALLY helpful to you, and for a VERY discounted price whenever possible, while at the same time making sure that I give you lots of additional free resources.

CHAPTER 1: INTRODUCTION

"Whether you think you can, or you think you can't, you are right."

- Henry Ford

1. Why offline marketing is still so effective

Everyone these days seems to be focused on promoting their business on social media, SEO (search engine optimization), or through other online methods. These strategies do work fantastically, and I myself use them with tremendous success. But offline marketing can still get you very far, especially since most people over-focus on online promotion of their businesses, it leaves the offline marketing techniques with less competition, which is great for you.

Offline marketing even has a number of strengths and advantages over online marketing. One of the main advantages that offline marketing has over online marketing is that in many of the offline marketing tactics, you get to meet people face to face, and forge a real human connection and a relationship. That is so much more powerful than having people find you online and click links, read text, see your little thumbnail photo, at at best watch your video.

In offline marketing, you can look people in the eyes, forge much stronger relationships, get people's trust, and have a chance to build a long-term business relationship with many people you meet. And not only will your sales conversion rate be higher after you get people's trust, but those new business relationships can give you value for years or even decades to come.

Some of the challenges that offline marketing has is that it doesn't scale like online marketing does. In online marketing, you can get hundreds, thousands, or even millions of people to come in contact with your work. But in offline marketing it takes a long time to talk to and convince many people to engage with your business.

Nevertheless, you can still accomplish quite a bit with offline marketing. It is still very effective, and in this book I will explain to you how you can get the most out of some of the most common offline marketing techniques.

2. Body language (nonverbal) sales communication

When you begin implementing the tactics in this book, you will immediately begin to meet many people in person, and talking to them. But did you know that up to 80% of all communication with your sales prospects can be nonverbal? In addition to communicating with the things you actually say, you also communicate with your body posture and positioning, your eyes, your hands, facial expressions, and the speed and tone of your voice?

Let's start with eye contact. Eye contact is something that subconsciously builds trust between people. Of course, don't be creepy with your eye contact and aggressively stare at people in the hope that you will build better eye contact. Over-doing eye contact can be very negative and put people off. Not having enough eye contact can make people feel like you are lying to them. But if you have just the right amount of positive eye contact, it can be very powerful during your conversations with people because it will subconsciously work to bring the two of you close during the conversation. Additionally, when you tell a story, and you get to some exciting part of that story, you can also emphasize the important parts of that story with the expressiveness of your eyes, which can often make your points and your storytelling much more effective. This is especially useful when you try to get people to imagine how much better your products or services can make their lives.

The next important aspect of your nonverbal communication is your body positioning and posture. Generally, you want to accomplish two things. You want to always appear open and comfortable. But you also want to mimic your sales prospect's body language. Salespeople often talk about mimicking voice, tone and body language of their sales prospects because it helps the sales prospects feel more comfortable and like the salesperson since the salesperson is just like they are.

You should also be mindful of your overall energy level. If the person you are talking to is low-energy and maybe a little bit skeptical of doing business with you, you don't want to be too energetic. Instead, you want to come down to their energy level, and in a normal and calm conversation build trust and rapport. On the other hand, if the person you are talking to has a lot of energy and excitement, you have to match their energy and help them keep building up the excitement.

You should do the same mimicking and matching of your prospect's speed and tone of voice. People like other people who are like them. They feel like those people are on their level and develop more trust towards them.

There are whole books devoted to nonverbal communication so there is a lot more to this. Nevertheless, these are your basic nonverbal body language tools to build immediate rapport with people you meet.

3. Your business pitch

In your offline marketing you will be meeting many people and building rapport with them. The next thing to have in your offline marketing toolbox is a business pitch that clearly and effectively explains your business that you can use whenever someone asks you what your business does (which will be very often).

When you talk about your company, you want to be brief and extremely clear. This helps people quickly understand your business and ask more questions if they are interested.

Here is a template for how you can explain your company very clearly at a high level in about 30 seconds. There are 3 to 5 main points you need to cover based on how much you want to divulge.

1) I am (planning/started/growing) a company (fill in your company name)

2) Which is a (website? physical store? mobile app? restaurant?)

3) For (fill in your target audience here).

4) The company aims to (fill in what is the purpose of the company, or what does it do for the target audience)

5) By (explain what the company will do differently or uniquely)

Credit for template: This template comes from Adeo Ressi from the Founders Institute.

Here are a few examples of business pitches using this template.

Example for a restaurant: I am considering opening a high end Italian restaurant in downtown London because there are currently no such restaurants there, and mine will bring the unique and Italian flavor of Italy to the heart of England.

Example for a website: I recently launched a website for people who like to work on classic cars. The website has articles and videos with tutorials for how to work on cars.

Example for a gardening company: I am in the planning stages of opening a residential lawn care and gardening company in San Francisco which will focus on providing the best customer experience with the lowest prices.

Example for a technology business: I am in the planning stages of mobile apps company in New York. The company will create mobile apps that help people create business plans on their mobile devices.

See how simple and clear these pitches are? They aren't meant to get people excited about your company just yet. All they are meant to do is to clearly explain what you do so that the other person can understand what your business is, and perhaps ask follow up questions.

Also notice that some of the example pitches are just one or two sentences, and can be said in under 10 seconds so that the conversation keeps flowing. Now let me explain how to structure your sales pitch so that people get excited about doing business with your company, and actually buy from you.

4. Your sales pitch

If you want to get someone excited about doing business with you, and you want to aggressively (in a good way) pitch your business to them, you must get them really excited from your very first sentence. Unlike your basic business pitch where you just have to make it clear what your business does, if you want to sell, you must also get someone excited about what they will be getting. When people buy, all they care about is what's in it for them.

Understanding this, the very first line of your sales pitch must be either some amazing promise (I will get to this in a second) or a qualifying question (I will get to this in a second also).

Let me explain what I mean by asking a qualifying question. This is a question meant to make whoever you are selling to feel like you understand what they need, and can provide the answer because you really understand the kind of a situation in which they find themselves in. Here are some examples:

If selling a weight loss product, the qualifying question would be: have you tried all the diets and exercise routines out there, but nothing has worked?

Most people would answer yes to that in their minds, and get more engaged with whatever you are about to tell them.

If selling a book about marketing to entrepreneurs, the qualifying question would go something like this: have you been trying to promote your business in different ways, but are just not seeing the results you had hoped for?

Again, most small business owners would say yes to that question.

When making a sales pitch to people who have at least a tiny bit of patience, I like to start with a qualifying question. If I am making a sales pitch to people with absolutely no patience for any fluff, I immediately start with a big promise.

Now let me explain what I mean by making a big promise.

For example, if you are selling the same weight loss product, but want to come out with more of a bang with your pitch, and still be different enough from all the other products that didn't work, here is how your initial sentence might look like: lose 10 pounds in your first 30 days with our new research-based approach and the support of our trainers and dietitians who will create a unique program that fits your situation.

This may not be the best sales pitch opener in the world, but it accomplishes a few important things. It establishes credibility by noting research, and it expresses uniqueness in that the person will be helped with different kinds of professionals like trainers and dietitians.

If you are selling a marketing book, your initial opener can be something like this: this marketing book will give you time-tested and proven offline marketing strategies that will be effective in promoting your business and get clients.

Again, this isn't the greatest pitch in the world, but it does accomplish a few things. First, it offers a unique solution to a person's problem. Second, it establishes authority by offering proven and time-tested strategies.

By giving a big and unique promise as your very first sentence, your goal is to get the person interested enough to stick around to hear the rest of your sales pitch.

This is all a part of an age-old marketing tactic called AIDA which I will explain to you now. After learning about AIDA, you should use principles of AIDA with almost anything you try to sell in the future. It truly works, and you will get better and better results as you get better with AIDA after lots of practice.

AIDA stands for: Attention, Interest, Desire, Action.

In your sales pitch, you want to:

1) Grab a person's attention (A)
2) Then build and maintain their interest throughout your sales pitch (I)
3) As you keep their interest you should get them to desire whatever it is that you are selling (D)
4) The last part is for them to take action (A)

The first line of your pitch that I have been talking about so far is the "A" part of AIDA. This is where you must grab people's attention.

Now let's talk about keeping people's interests and inspiring their desires.

To keep people's attention and build their desire you must explain the BENEFITS and not FEATURES of the product or service you are selling, and invoke their imagination and positive emotions.

Benefits (in the weight loss example) are things like losing weight, looking better, and being sexier. These things are what people truly want. Features are things like diet plans, working with trainers and so on. No one dreams of having a diet plan. People dream of the benefit of their diet plan, which is to look better. And that is what you must focus on instead of the execution details.

The way you invoke people's positive emotions is by making them feel how challenging their current situation is, and helping them imagine how much better their lives would be after they got your product. Try to also use the word "you" as often as it can be used while still having your pitch sound well and make sense. The word "you" helps to get people to feel like your solution is truly for them, and begin imagining themselves getting the benefits of your product or service.

What we are talking about now is a field called Sales Copywriting. There are entire books written on this subject. A well-written sales pitch can help you increase sales by hundreds of percent. Let me give you actual examples of videos where this kind of a script helped me raise sales by hundreds of percent.

Watch the sales video for my big online marketing course and see how I use the ideas I just explained in that video. This video helped me double the sales for this course, which had already been selling well. The sales video should appear on top of the page here:

https://www.udemy.com/marketing-plan-strategy-become-a-great-marketer/

Here is another example of a video that helped me raise sales by hundreds of percent. The script for this video is exactly a model for the script of your own product or service. Use it as an example for how to craft your sales pitch:

https://www.udemy.com/how-to-create-grow-a-mobile-app-iphone-android-business/

If you need help crafting the pitch of your product or service, I can help you do that and increase your sales conversion. Readers of this book get a very discounted rate, starting at $5 for a 15 minute coaching call where I help you with your marketing (*yes that is $5*) through this service:

https://www.fiverr.com/genadinik/send-you-the-digital-copy-of-my-marketing-plan-book-reach-one-million-people--3

NOTE: I am sorry for suggesting a paid service to you right in the middle of the book, and especially in the beginning of it, but this is the sort of an offer which should pay for itself many times over, and almost immediately, so I thought it was ok to add here. Also, in the end of the book I have a number of free gifts for you to balance out this paid offer, so take advantage of those as well.

Now let's get back to your sales pitch. Once you have gotten people's attention, kept their interest and built up their desire, you must get them to take action. This action part is the last part of the AIDA process. The action is often to buy something or to sign up for something. Instructing people to engage in the way you need them to engage is crucial. If you don't tell them what you need them to do, many of them won't do it. It is that simple.

If you take people through the AIDA path effectively, it will make your sales pitches work amazingly well for you. When I was first starting out with this, while it made sense in theory, it wasn't immediately clear how I can actually create such sales pitches on my own. But over time, I have become better and better with it, and so will you. Keep practicing it, and you will do great over time.

5. Key to your marketing success

I want to finish this first chapter with just one quick note, mentioning that to succeed in almost any marketing strategy, you must have persistence and consistency. Whatever you try, if you are starting out, things might not always immediately begin working to bring you clients.

If at first things don't work, don't feel discouraged, and don't quit. Like all other entrepreneurs, you just have to persevere. Consistency and persistence will be the keys to your success. Keep trying to figure out what went wrong, and keep fixing it. Over time, you will find success with your marketing attempts.

6. Focus on retaining customers long-term

I realize that you may be very curious and excited about finding ways to get new customers. But did you ever hear a common business saying that it is easier to sell to an existing customer than it is to find a new customer?

Not only do repeat and long-term customers obviously spend more money with your business, but they help you in many additional indirect ways. Long-term customers are more likely to leave positive online reviews which will in turn help you draw more customers. Long-term customers are also much more likely to recommend your business to their friends, and many friends over time.

The common strategies to get people to become long-term customers are:

- Collect email addresses of your customers and write a regular newsletter with occasional announcements and discounts
- Have a multiple-product product line to let people buy additional products
- Have follow-on services for products people can buy like maintenance or part replacement
- Sell consumable products that are needed on a regular basis
- Sell subscription-based products or services
- Provide an amazing experience to your customers and delight them into coming back
- Provide great customer service that helps people build trust and positive emotions towards your business

7. Practical: how to get your business cards and flyers made

Later in this book I will cover how to promote your business with business cards, flyers and other print materials. You might wonder where to get these items actually designed and printed so I'll cover a few options that you have.

If you want to do the design and printing online, I recommend a website called VistaPrint.com which is where I print my business cards and flyers. They have thousands of existing designs available that you can choose from. You can create the design and get it printed for you right on that site.

If you want to have a custom design, you can do that on VistaPrint as well, although it will be a little bit expensive. To get a cheap custom design, take look at Fiverr.com where you can get business cards and flyers designed for you for as low as just $5.

Of course, as these strategies succeed for you and you will need to print more and more business cards, flyers and other printed marketing materials, you can approach local print shops to see whether they can work out a deal for a significant discount printing in bulk for you. The designs they can print can be the designs that you found on VistaPrint or got custom made on Fiverr.

Generally, the ultimate design is something that most people outsource because let's face it, most of us are not designers. It is easy to get the flyers designed for you and printed. The challenging part is to have what's printed on it resonate with people.

CHAPTER 2: OFFLINE MARKETING STRATEGIES

"Do what you can, with what you have, where you are."
- Theodore Roosevelt

1. How to get yourself appearances on the radio and podcasts

I personally have gotten over 50 podcast and radio show appearances within one year (and over 100 over time) for myself just by using this website:

http://www.radioguestlist.com

I even have an online course about how you can take the most advantage of this website here (and you can get this course as a **free** gift from me - I explain that at the end of this book):

https://www.udemy.com/how-i-got-50-podcast-appearances-using-radioguestlist/

Once you sign up for the free account on the radioguestlist.com website, every weekday they will send you a list of podcasts and radio shows which are looking for experts to interview. And you can pitch those radio show and podcast hosts to see whether they will want to interview you. You already have some pitch tools in your toolbox from chapter one, which should be a good guide for how to pitch radio stations as well.

In the online course which I mentioned that you can get for free from me, I explain and walk you through exactly how I pitched radio show and podcast hosts to get 50+ interviews for myself in just 1 year.

2. 3 ways to get business referrals

I put 3 different ways to get referrals in this section because there are many ways to get referrals, and many of them are actually not related to one another. For example, you might get a referral from an existing customer or you might get a referral from another business with whom you might have a business relationship with. These are both called referrals, but the strategies to get these referrals are pretty different. So in this section, I'll cover all the different ways to get offline referrals.

Let's start with how to get referrals from your existing customers, and get them to invite their friends. This is also what some people sometimes refer to as *word of mouth marketing*.

The most important thing when it comes to getting customer referrals is your product quality. If your product or service is amazing, and leaves your customers thrilled and feeling like they just got an amazing value, they will naturally talk about your product or services with friends, and recommend it.

But even if your customers truly love your product or service, they won't recommend it to friends that often. There just isn't enough for them in it. For that reason, you must always give them incentives, and the incentives must be for the current customer, and any new potential customers they might bring. Let me give you an example.

If you offer a customer 20% OFF their next purchase if they bring a friend, there is not enough incentive for the friend to try out your business. And if you give 20% OFF to the friend, there is not enough incentive for the current customer to make the recommendation because there is nothing in it for the current customer. But if you give 20% OFF (or whatever other discount) to both of them, then suddenly, the current customer will have enough incentive to invite friends, and the friends will know that they will be getting a good deal, and will come more readily.

This is how you maximize your social referrals: through very high quality services and products, and double incentives. Don't just rely on people to recommend your business to others. Control, influence, and maximize it with correct incentives.

Another way to get referrals is to get professional referrals. This strategy is completely different from getting customer referrals. To get professional referrals, you need to build relationships with businesses in your industry which can refer clients to you, and you can refer clients to them.

For example, the medical community has this nailed down pat. If you go to a general physician, and he spots a skin problem, he recommends you to go to a specific skin care doctor. If you have a foot problem, he recommends a foot doctor. If he thinks some medicine can help you, he recommends that medicine. Being on that doctor's recommendation list can drive a lot of businesses.

This is what you have to do as well. If you are a mechanic, build relationships with companies that clean cars, paint cars, sell and install fancy rims or car stereo systems, and so on. If their customers ever have their cars break, they can refer those customers to you. And if your customers ever need a paint job or ask about car stereo systems, you can refer those people to those companies. This way you develop a professional network of companies who refer clients to one another, and boost each other's business.

The third way you get referrals is to pay other companies for the leads that they send you, or pay a commission after one of the leads they sent you becomes a paid customer. Paying is a very powerful way to incentivize other companies in your niche to send you leads and referrals.

3. Promoting your business by networking and with business cards

Networking is a lifestyle and a mindset. Wherever you are in any social situation, as long as you keep it socially appropriate, you are networking. Don't confine your networking to just networking events.

You should always have at least 3-5 business cards with you in your wallet. If you go to a networking event bring 30. If you present at a networking or business event, bring 50 business cards just in case.

Now let me explain how to make people want your business cards. Whenever you talk to people at networking events or any time in real life, don't just start going on and on about how great your business is, how much greater it will be, and what a great entrepreneur you are. And don't proceed to give people a business card right away.

Instead of being overly salesy, what you must do is to first establish at least some sort of a relationship with whoever you are talking to. One great way to do that is to ask the person you are talking to about what they do for work. When they answer, listen actively, and follow up with insightful questions or suggestions for help or suggestions for people you can connect that person to who might be able to help.

Let me give you a few guidelines on what to ask people to get them to open up to you, and build trust and rapport. Tap into people's emotions. We are all emotional beings (yes, even men are emotional). We all have hopes, aspirations, fears, anxieties, ambition, happiness, etc. What you must do it get out of bland fact-based conversation and get into a conversation that leads people to happy emotions.

Here is an example of a question sequence that will have a very high chance to make you sound intelligent, get people to open up to you, associate their positive emotions with their interactions with you, and build that immediate trust:

You: What do you do?
Other person: whatever job they do
You: what is your favorite part of your work? OR what inspired you to get into this?
Other person: some answer

You: what will it mean for you to truly succeed in what you do? Do you have a plan to get there? (this will get them to daydream a little bit)
You: when are you most excited in your day?

Do you see how these questions you might ask are ones that tap into giving you more or less emotional answers which are positive? Also, almost no one asks those insightful questions. Most people just say something like "oh, you do xyz, that's awesome" which is followed by awkward silence.

Your conversation would be much more interesting and engaging. And after that exchange, the person you are talking to will want to know what such an interesting person as yourself does, and they will ask you what you do.

BOOM! Now this is your time to shine. You already stand out above the crowd to the person with whom you are talking. Now, just give a brilliant pitch of your business to make you and the business look like a million bucks (remember making your pitch in chapter one?), give them a way to engage with your business if there is any synergy between the two of you (if not, then what are you still doing there at that point?), and suggest exchanging business cards if the other person hasn't already suggested exchanging business cards.

Let me give you a few tips for what to do with business cards that you collect. Carry a pen with you so that as soon as you step away, you can write down some of the key points of your exchange with the person with whom you just talked to, and what you must follow up about. Within the next 30 minutes, you will forget half of the conversation. Ideally, the next day after meeting, you should email them to build on your conversation, and with suggestions with next steps if any.

As a rule of thumb, always follow up in the next day or two on every business card that you collect. Also, try to follow them on Twitter on connect on LinkedIn. Those are the minimal things you can do to keep in touch, and collect positive long-term business contacts.

4. Join a local press club

Every large city has a local press club. Outside the press world this is a little known strategy, but it can pay you amazing dividends. A press club is where journalists and press professionals meet and network.

What you can do is come to the press club events, and volunteer as an expert "source" which is the industry term for someone who contributes an expert opinion to an article. If those journalists use your expert opinion, you can get free publicity for you and your business in local newspapers, even larger publications, and sometimes even TV.

If you don't know how to find a local press club, go to Google.com and search this:
"press club in city_name" where city_name is the big city in which you live or the nearest big city to the one in which you live. Small cities don't usually have press clubs so you will have to search for the nearest big city to where you live.

Once you find your local press club, go to their website, look up the next time they meet, the requirements to attend, and then go ahead and attend that press club meeting. Come ready with your business cards, business pitch, positive body language signs and all your other strategies to get the most out of the connections you make there.

If you are in New York, for example, here is the local website for the press club:

https://www.newyork**pressclub**.org

5. When to hire a publicist to get you more publicity

This is the only strategy in this book which will be expensive to execute. A publicist or a publicity agency can get you really fantastic publicity and exposure, but they are quite expensive. In United States, it would be rare to find a reasonably good publicist for under $5,000/month, and agencies usually charge around $10,000/month on retainer, which means that you can't just hire them for one month, but must commit to at least 3-6 months as minimum.

This immediately eliminates most small business owners, but as soon as you begin having extra marketing budget, this is something to begin considering since this would get you great branding and direct sales.

The good news is that if you master RadioGuestList and join your local press club, you might just get so much publicity for your business that you won't even need a publicist. That is what I hope that you can accomplish for yourself.

6. Where to plaster your logo and website

Depending on the kind of business you have, different places make sense for printing your logo, business name and website URL. As a business owner, you probably wouldn't mind if the entire earth was covered with your logo. So there has to be a limit somewhere. Let's explore where it makes sense to print your logo, business name and website URL.

The first place on which you should put your logo and website URL is...YOURSELF! Get nice t-shirts and hats made that you wouldn't mind wearing. Give those t-shirts and hats to your staff as well.

If you have a local business like roofing, handyman, restaurant, or anything similar, you can also put the logo and website URL on the sides of your car, and on your bumper. If your bumper sticker is funny, it will get people's attention and stand out because typically when people are looking at your bumper, they are bored in traffic, and if you give them a little bit of extra entertainment, they will engage.

Some people also like to have pens, key-chains or other small items made with their logos on those items. I am not a fan of this strategy if your budget is tight. The only way I would pursue that strategy for a small business that is just starting out is to think about what your ideal customer does regularly, make an item that helps them with that, and put your logo/URL on that item. Then, since there is a cost to having those items made, only give that item for free to people who you think are very good potential candidates to someday become customers.

Sometimes you can charge people a few dollars to buy these items if those items are actually cool and useful. This can be nice because you get to have people pay you a little bit to advertise your company.

If your business is a local business, you can try promoting your business or URL on a billboard if that makes financial sense for you. Typically billboards have contact information for the company who owns them, and you can call and inquire how much a billboard ad would cost, and try to negotiate a rate that would make sense for you.

7. Promoting your business with flyers

Many first-time entrepreneurs and marketers choose the tactic of handing out flyers as one of their very initial attempts at promoting their business.

It is worth taking a moment for a word of caution. Passing out flyers is fine for some businesses, but completely useless for many others. The problem many entrepreneurs run into is that they don't know which kinds of businesses this works for, and try it regardless, simply because it is one of the first marketing strategies that occur to them.

In fact, here is a test to see whether you are falling into this trap. Let me ask you what your marketing strategy will be. Think for 10 seconds...OK, you came up with it? Does it sounds like this:

"I will promote my business with Facebook, Twitter, business cards and flyers."

If your strategy for promotion sounds something close to this, you are like about 80% of first-time marketers. That's OK, but you just need to improve your strategy a little (or a lot) bit more.

Here are the kinds of businesses that can benefit from passing out flyers: restaurants during lunch time, local stores and services promoting special offers, and events.

Relatively few other types of businesses truly benefit from passing out flyers. So if you don't have a business like the one mentioned above, think twice about this particular strategy because printing out flyers is not cheap. There are printing costs and the costs of having someone stand and pass them out.

If you are not certain about whether this strategy will work for you, at the end of this book, one of the gifts I have for you is that you can email me, and ask me questions. So just email me, explaining that you got this book, and tell me a little bit about your business, and I can explain whether marketing with flyers will work for your kind of business. I might even suggest some marketing strategies that I think would work really well for your unique business once I learn a little bit about it.

Here are some instructions for how to create and hand out flyers.

Before you even make the flyers, make the offer on them something amazing because that will be the main difference maker for whether people will engage with the flyers or not.

For example, a 50% discount on something they don't know that they need is much more exciting than a 10% discount. You can make it just a first-time customer offer since a 50% discount is not sustainable, or a different kind of an exciting offer since this is just an example. But whatever you do, make the offer seem like truly great value. It will make a significant difference in the success of that entire flier-marketing campaign. Remember AIDA? Well, the offer is your first A in AIDA. This is where you must grab a person's attention so that the details of the flier can build interest and desire.

Once you have a clear good offer, make it very visible on the flier, or make sure that the person handing out flyers is friendly, animated and vocal enough to make people take the flyers and give the flyers a real consideration.

8. Promoting your business with events and workshops

Promoting a business with workshops or events is my single most favorite offline marketing strategy.

Events can generate an extra source of revenue for your business, improve your branding and customer awareness directly, or through publicity that events can generate. And, of course, the attendees of the events can become leads and eventual customers for your main business.

You can create an event series for whatever makes sense for your business. You can entertain, educate or create a community around whatever subject area your business is in.

Let me give you a few examples of events that are used for different kinds of businesses. When I had a hiking business, I generated revenue and drove leads by putting on really exciting themed hikes to unique places. When technology companies want to raise awareness for their products, they put on events with technology presenters, and draw a tech audience. These tend to be groups with as few as 15 people to large conferences with thousands of attendees. If you sell a service, you can start an educational workshop on how to do that service. From that kind of a workshop, some people who try what you teach on your own and fail, will be likely to consider hiring you.

You must come up with a great event theme, and then promote the event. You can promote the events on social media, your website, or meetup.com which is the world's biggest event website that can get you many attendees. And, of course, you can generate revenue from events by directly charging for attendance, or up-selling your company's products or services to the attendees.

If you are interested in putting on events to give your business a boost, you can take my event planning and marketing online course for free since I offer one free online course of mine for free to readers of this book. Read more of that in the free gifts section at the end of this book. If you prefer learning by reading, here is a link to my event planning and marketing book on Amazon:

http://www.amazon.com/Event-Planning-Management-Successful-successful-ebook/dp/B017T2B2XK

(but better, take my course since you can get it for free)

9. Door to door marketing

Door to door marketing is another one of those promotional strategies that only works for some businesses and products.

Often, the kinds of products that sell well with door to door marketing are visual products that are not too expensive relative to the affluence level of the neighborhood in which you will be selling. Ideally it could be something they could use for the home. For example, I once knew of a home painter who simply walked around affluent or middle class neighborhoods and whenever he saw a home that could have used a new paint job, he would simply knock on the door and give his sales pitch. That was very effective for him, especially as he became very good at his sales pitch.

Remember your sales pitch from chapter one and the points on body language? This is where these must really work for you. If you knock on someone's door and they see that you are trying to sell them something, their initial reaction might be annoyance and irritation. In many cases you only have a few sentences to perk their interest. If you don't, they will just close the door on you.

This is why having a nicely presented visual product that might get their attention (remember A as the attention in AIDA?), and an effective sales pitch can really help make or break your sales campaign and give you a good sales conversion.

Another thing you want to try to do is to do your door to door marketing during a time of the day when the person you are selling to is at home. If you are selling something that requires the head of household's decision to buy, you want to go in the evening. And if you are selling something that requires a stay at home mom's decision to buy, then you might want to go earlier in the day.

The difference between randomly trying to sell something and using a correct sales pitch with the right script with the AIDA structure in literally hundreds of percent. So make sure that your sales pitch is practiced, well scripted and works.

And keep in mind that this particular way to promote your business or products is going to have a lot of rejection. That rejection can give you low confidence. Try to catch yourself on that thought if you find yourself feeling a lack of confidence. You just have to persevere. Rejection is very much a part of sales. But if you persevere, and eventually become very good at sales, you will be able to sell anything, and it will give you a boost for the rest of your career.

10. Guerilla marketing and publicity stunts

Here is how the father of Guerrilla Marketing, Jay Conrad Levinson describes guerrilla marketing:

"I'm referring to the soul and essence of guerrilla marketing which remain as always - achieving conventional goals, such as profits and joy, with unconventional methods, such as investing energy instead of money.

To me, this means using a lot of creativity and a unique approach to promote whatever it is you are promoting. Also, to me, this is very close to Seth Godin's purple cow concept. The idea behind the concept of the Purple Cow is that since a purple cow would be something very unusual (since it doesn't exist), most people would stop to take a closer look at it if they saw one.

The idea is that you have to bring uniqueness to whatever you do, and that uniqueness will get you to stand out.

Now let me explain what publicity stunts are. They are related to guerrilla marketing. Publicity stunts are things that you specifically do to get so much attention that eventually press picks it up. To get attention you have to do something very unusual, out of the ordinary, and attention-grabbing. A classic example of this is when someone was selling people parts of the Brooklyn bridge. If you are not familiar with the Brooklyn bridge, it is a very iconic bridge, much like the Golden Gate bridge in terms of its fame.

So how can some individual be selling parts of the Brooklyn bridge? Don't they need to have permission, or to own it first? And how can they sell an entire bridge? Rumors and stories quickly spread about the person who was selling the Brooklyn bridge, and got enough attention from people to get press coverage and become such a large story that years later I am noting it here. But really, what was happening was that during regular maintenance of the bridge, little chips of the rock from the bridge would fall, and one guy would pick up those pieces, and sell those pieces as parts of the Brooklyn bridge. Not only was he getting free product inventory, but he also generated a lot of press for himself.

Try to think of how to do something that creates a good and exciting headline for whatever you are doing, which will grab people's attention.

11. Classifieds newspaper ads

Classified ads can be purchased in local or national newspapers. As you can imagine, the reach and cost would vary greatly. Local papers would charge you from one to few hundred dollars, and national newspapers can be as costly as tens of thousands of dollars per a single ad. You can also advertise in daily vs. weekly publications. Obviously weekly publications will be cheaper.

What you must do is experiment with ads that will work in a local weekly publication since they are the cheapest. To maximize your experimentation, you can try advertising in many different local newspapers at the same time to see which ad has better conversion. Once you find an ad type and copy (copy is the sales text you write on your ad) that converts, you can advertise in bigger and bigger newspapers.

One challenge is measuring how your classifieds ads actually convert. Many of your customers never tell you how they found your business. So you might never know if someone came from a classifieds ad. What you must do is give people either unique phone number line to call, or a unique discount code or a unique website page to visit so that you can know that everyone coming or calling through that is from a specific classifieds ad.

Another thing to keep in mind is what kind of a demographic you will be reaching. Very few kinds of people actually read classifieds ads. Most of the people who read newspapers these days tend to be over the age of 40 or 45 and older. They may also be the kinds of people who resist technological change.

12. Direct snail mail advertising

Even in this digital age, you still get companies mailing you physical letters for promotions, right? There are fewer such mailings, and they typically only come from a few types of companies. That should be a sign for you as to what kind of companies can be effectively promoted with direct snail mail, and whether your business fits into the profile of such a company.

Generally, if your business is a commonly used local business like a store or a restaurant, you can try to send people in your neighborhood promotions by regular snail mail, or slip flyers or brochures under their doors.

Keep in mind that there is a cost to sending or handing out every brochure, direct mailing or flyer. So only promote your business this way if it is something that gets you results and you can measure those results in the ways that I described earlier.

Rule of thumb: if you can't measure results of any paid promotion, you truly have no idea whether that promotion is profitable or whether you are losing money on it.

13. Cold calling and phone sales

To start with cold calling you need a great sales pitch, and luckily if you have gotten to this part of the book, you already have one.

The next thing you need is to figure out who will do the calling. I have hired telemarketers on Fiverr.com in the past who can call 15 numbers for about $5, but that is the cheapest it can go.

When cold calling, you must have the conversation mapped out in advance to account for the most common answers someone can give you, and have a response to every non-optimal answer.

Finding the numbers to call can also be a challenge. If you are selling to businesses, their phone numbers are easy to collect because they all have websites where they readily post their phone numbers.

If you are calling individual consumers, there are two strategies for getting their phone numbers. The first is going to annoy people in a major way, but it will enable you to reach thousands of people. It is by pre-loading the phone book's list of phone numbers to an automated software that automatically calls people one by one, and tells them about your offer. 95% of the people who will be called will absolutely hate that you are sending them automated voice messages and automated phone calls, but a small percentage of the people whom you call this way will engage with whatever you are offering. The other way to get people's phone numbers is to buy lists of consumer phone numbers for consumers who fit the target demographics of the kinds of consumers that you are targeting.

14. Storefront without a storefront

A storefront is something that brick and mortar businesses have. It is a part of the building that faces a street with a window. This window allows people who walk by the business to peek inside, learn about the business, and hopefully take an interest. In many cases the window of the store is the A of AIDA as it is meant to grab people's attention.

If you are opening a physical location for your business, a really big part of the decision as to where to open it would be to find a location which has a big storefront on a street which gets a lot of foot traffic.

But what if you don't have a storefront in case your business is a website or another business which doesn't have a physical location other than your home or some tucked-away office?

If you don't have a readily available storefront, you can artificially manufacture one by setting up a cart or a stand or a truck with big signs, logos and your URL somewhere on a busy street with lots of passer-by foot traffic. This way you can actually make some sales while getting many people who don't initially engage to at least notice and become familiar with your business. That familiarity will increase the chances that next time they pass by and see your business they might engage.

15. Setting up a cart or a stand or selling at flea markets or fairs

Taking off from the previous section's idea of setting up a storefront, you can also try to sell your products or promote your business at flea markets, fairs or similar events. If you are not familiar with what flea markets are, they are basically large places where many small businesses gather to sell or promote their goods to people who are looking for unique items or discounts. Every large city has fairs and flea markets.

Try to find what fairs or flea markets are going on in the nearby cities and towns near you, and try to promote whatever your business sells there.

All you need to do is invest in a portable chair, table and nice signs so that your business looks attractive, and you will be able to drum up some sales anywhere you set up your basic stand.

The End

Best of luck promoting your business! I wish you amazing success in everything you do, and really hope that the strategies in this book bring you tremendous profits.

WHAT DID YOU THINK OF THIS BOOK?

I want to hear from you. If you liked the book or didn't, please email me your thoughts to my email alex.genadinik@gmail.com

FURTHER FREE RESOURCES AND DISCOUNTS

FREE GIFTS FOR YOU AND EXTRA RESOURCES

Gift 1: I will give you one free online business/marketing course of YOUR choosing and huge discounts on any additional courses.

I teach over 60 online courses on business and marketing. Just for you, I will give you one for absolutely free, and you choose which one. Browse my full list of courses and email me telling me which course you want, and I will send you a free coupon!

Here is my full list of courses:

https://www.udemy.com/user/alexgenadinik/

Just send me an email to alex.genadinik@gmail.com and tell me that you got this book, and which of my courses you would like for free, and I will send you a coupon code to get that course for free.

Want any additional courses? To get any other course for almost free, use the discount coupon code: thankyouforreading

Gift: 2: Get my Android business apps for free.

My apps come as a 4-app course and on Android I have free versions of each!

Free business plan app:
https://play.google.com/store/apps/details?id=com.problemio&hl=en

Free marketing app:
https://play.google.com/store/apps/details?id=com.marketing&hl=en

Free app on fundraising and making money:
https://play.google.com/store/apps/details?id=make.money&hl=en

Free business idea app:

https://play.google.com/store/apps/details?id=business.ideas&hl=en

I am sorry, but my iPhone apps are not free and it isn't easy to make them free. But if you are interested, they start at just $0.99 and you can browse all my paid apps on my website: http://www.problemio.com

Gift 3: Free business advice

If you have questions about your events, your overall business, or anything mentioned in this book, email me at alex.genadinik@gmail.com and I will be happy to help you. Just please keep two things in mind:

1) Remind me that you got this book and that you are not just a random person on the Internet.
2) Please make the questions clear and short. I love to help, but I am often overwhelmed with work, and always short on the time that I have available.

COMPLETE LIST OF MY BOOKS

If you enjoyed this book, check out my Amazon author page to see the full list of my books:
http://www.amazon.com/Alex-Genadinik/e/B00I114WEU

VERY AFFORDABLE BUSINESS COACHING FROM ME

Here is a way you can get really affordable business and marketing coaching from me, in a one on one Skype call where you and I discuss everything about your business. I know this gig talks about SEO strategy, but we can talk about anything you want regarding your business. The key is that you and I get on a Skype call with the gig that you buy with this link:

https://www.fiverr.com/genadinik/help-you-plan-an-seo-strategy

DID YOU ENJOY THE BOOK?

If you liked the book, I would sincerely appreciate it if you left a review about your experience on Amazon.

And if you didn't enjoy it, or were expecting to get different things out of it, please email me at alex.genadinik@gmail.com and I will be happy to add/edit material in this book to make it better.

Thank you for reading and please keep in touch!

ABOUT THE AUTHOR

Alex Genadinik is a software engineer, an entrepreneur, and a marketer. Alex is a 3-time best selling Amazon author, and the creator of the Problemio.com business apps which are some of the top mobile apps for planning and starting a business with 1,000,000 downloads across iOS, Android and Kindle. Alex has a B.S in Computer Science from San Jose State University.

Alex is also a prominent online teacher, and loves to help entrepreneurs achieve their dreams.

Printed in Great Britain
by Amazon

58296824R00027